I Could Be Dreaming

Kerri Moore

ISBN No. 978-0-9572395-0-0
Published by Kerri Moore
With kind sponsorship from
Taylor John's Music and Arts Centre Ltd
and The Pea Pod Collective

Printed by Proprint
Remus House
Woodston
Peterborough PE2 9BF

I was born 1964. My name is Kerri Moore

I dedicate this book to my mother,
And brother.

Contents

Homespun

Homespun and threadbare,
A whistler on the wind,
Crudely recreated,
The flam; the fragrant
Flair, Tantalus.

Ignominiously, he
Takes his shame,
And makes ideals of it,
To appertain,
Life is a living glory,

A moving story,
He mouths the reed,
Sirrah, he deems,
Sinuously, his dreams,
Redeemed.

He leaps like a salamander,
Into the fires.
The generate become genesis
To Sion, make inherited the land.
Of those who dance,
In silk spun shrouds.

Midnight Prayer

Love live long,
In the heart of thee.
Why ever reason,
Space and nautical being?
Transessence, could be so shallow,
Or deep, and my own invention.

I could reason, nonsense!
See the meaning in contrary,
Misunderstandings, of need,
I could grieve my own calling,
Transplant the seed;
A crowd o' gathering muses.

To shout or even scream,
Call out my own name;
I could believe in namesake!
All in all, that which is personal,
So unaware and assumed,
Maria, behind the wire!

The Outlaw's Song

The mortal thread,
Timeless,
Ageless.

As can die in a man's heart,
His vain heart's desire, his destiny.
Make him a nobleman;
A stranger,
A stranger.

Madonna . . .
Do you believe?
. . . In gardens of dream.

This is the desert of my song,
These my silent breaths;
Make me a beggar of faith,
Take my heart and breath away.

In thoughts I stumble
To make question, in myself,
There is love on your face,
My love, my exile, my peace.

And he who calls himself love,
Static and conscience,
Becomes a fearful master,
My heart is as cold as a wild beast.
My love is tamed,
And there is no one to blame; mercy!
My potions, my love, my steed,
Outlaw you know me well.

The Invisible Form Of Christ

Leonardo knew Christ.
He knew his cheekbones,
And photographic quality.
He knew fame,
To be his own prodigy.

Will you relax!
I'll get your good side!
I'll make you an idyll!
Be still now!
It'll be over in a flash.

Immortalised,
Nevertheless, nevermore.
I have reproductive ability . . .
I can imagine you,
In a pose like this!

Leonardo lay down;
His leg and arm outstretched,
In a pose, he was outlined,
Communicating,
With his own beliefs.

The Rebellion

It was the serpent,
Spoke his first words,
To Homage!
In the first frame of knowledge;
Spinning his intrigue,
And more,
His captivity.

A rope so bound,
Seven souls,
Sisters,
Who spun their songs to Pan;
In vain, they sang,
'Destiny so fair,
Hail, Mort,
His captivity.'

Then, rapturous souls,
Exploded, and made streams
Of their sorrows,
Sang, the sanguine! In rivers,
Underground to praise Mort,
That right is just
All the more,
To captivity!

The Heavens

Interweave my body
Into the inner scene,
Of my dreams.
I speak of Heaven,
I know you do not like to hear of these things.

It is not harbour, or grief,
Nor magic to believe.
Not in loss, but life, an acquisition,
Of honour, excitedly,
Patiently, to know, the day will come . . .

The poet, is lumbered as such;
With the sun, the sky, the sea,
Blake, his abacus, his prophesy.
You did believe then,
In the sun, the sky, and the sea.

The Unknown

Truth is not belief,
Belief is not truth,
No matter how far, or how far
You see it,
Ahead of you,
No matter how far you see,
The future is unknown.

But isn't that how we survive?
Isn't it how
When the moment comes
The surprise in union,
When you find happiness
Even if briefly,
Even fleetingly?

Maybe you rise,
In a love, in a land of love,
Isn't life a surprise?
When find, you're in love
With the world, isn't it . . .
The most beautiful thing there is?
Is it the most beautiful thing?

Isn't it wonderful? And doesn't it
Keep on rising,
In your insides?
You look at love,
And see it ahead of you,
The future of love,
The future is yours, life is yours.

Love is yours, life is yours

The Houses Of Parliament

She is tight-lipped,
Like an assumption,
She trades life in Ecuador.

The opinions she squanders,
Like pearls cast before swine,
She deals treacherously.

The central nucleus, vibrates within,
The theme of bamboozle,
Bored with adornments.

Each persona, content of status,
Could suppose to propose,
Downfall to the man who will not take her hand.

She bathes in prejudice,
And keeps clean her guilt in poverty,
Keeps the secret under her skin.
She hoards belief in purpose,
To say life has no gift or sacrifice,
Except its debt to her universe.

Then takes she, her title,
Like a martyr, slightly undefined,
In her luxury and exploit.
Her children, borne of horses,
Make power, to perpetuate the engine,
And tame justification.
No more hours in the day,
Could ever reward you,
With her prosperity.

The Four Freedoms

> . . . of speech and expression,
> . . . of worship
> . . . from fear,
> . . . from want.

The law of contradiction,
Could footle in oration,
To sworn plutocracy,
In rise to quell its looting,
Longing for elevation,
Confounded by the profane,
Profundis prohibitions.

> A random birth, should justify
> A place in this systemised,
> Pietism, to gloat!
> Make ramshackle to rake-hell!
> Improvise the dream,
> Compromise, judicial, liege-man,
> His wife, stale mate.

Gather in a gold rush,
In lieu, the bottom dollar,
Is the martyr to the partisan,
Denied, the fundamental
Belief of equal worth.
Infidel of fidelity, hush,
It's money to the rumbling belly.

> Mete out the scourge,
> The outcry, pent, is liberation,
> Pay penance to the corrupted,
> Down cast by lacklustre,
> Modality is inured to selection,
> 'til lifeless, the day, mocks
> The day's timelessness

The Face Of Love

Fear has the power of many demons;
I could face any man,
But love,
I have fear of him.

He can tear the inside out,
He can make you speak of dreams,
He can tell you anything,
And that, you would believe.

He may have an angel's face,
But the heart of a devil,
Can feel you, deep, deep;
And you give to him, everything.

Then, when just you believe him most,
He can summon fear, summon demons,
He can imitate love,
And yes, I have fear of him.

Spectre

My body is floating,
I'm no survivor,
Pure penitent gloat.

It has no matter,
Or control,
My lost soul.
I am a dried river,
On which you float,
Forever.

I am not going to fall,
I'm not going
To need anyone, at all.

Untold manifold,
No sell out, unsold,
Limitless, speed.
A spectre,
The spectre bat,
The restored Christ.

Restrained, evirate,
A hollowed out seed pearl,
The rebuke of man.

No repent, no repine,
Guttersnipe,
Le Chevalier,
No repent,
The barefooted
Baptist, epiphyte.

The Bugle Call

Hunter, hunter!
Did you not convict her?
Of her major tragedies,
And modest gaucherie,
Her mediocre tendencies?

At Heaven's gate.
In antiquity,
Her deep impression,
Had languor of the winds,
And reedy laudation of stanzas.

False-hood, could plant his seed,
Murmuring a bubblin' potion,
In the night, the klutz of dawn,
Wake! We were dreaming.
The curtain call.

We make salute.
To freedom! To dying!
For the cause,
Sing now, of morning's glory,
From the darkness of sleep

The Valley

My blood ran cold, in the valley,
Where once, the harbour had warmed me,
I perch by the fireside of the sun,
A long winter night to come,
No story to tell, no grudge to kiss,
I whisper love to the wind.

The sharpened wit, the welcome brew,
I sang a song or two, about you,
In the smoke of a flame,
Burning and bellowing, your name;
Never did a tale we tell, so well,
To know love in the depths of hell!

I wish, my love, to be with you,
Free of borders, that bind me so,
In a land, unlearnt, I cannot speak,
In slight of tongue, or heritage;
To whom they belong,
These progressions of song

Stone Age Love

When we discovered love.
The place was in uproar,
Every man for himself!

God only knows the meaning,
Of feelings in uproar.
He didn't make man beg or kneel,
But he let him steal.

As if not to know,
Of consequence and derivation,
As if you didn't know,
It was chaos and beautiful.

And God only knows
In time and history,
When judgement and honesty,
Becomes the love of the heart!

Vera Cruz Harbour Boys

In the interstice,
Where injustice breeds her race,
The Vera Cruz harbour boys,
The translators,
The interpreters,

Space check.

In the dredges where the swaggers hang,
In suspense of refusal,
Or premonition.

Carve out the rhythm,
However small the step,
On the beach, on the south side,
I remember there, making love,
In the comfortable rivers of your fingers.

From your forefathers in Mexico,
In Venezuela and Santa Monica.
Today we set sail,
Toward the Adriatic,
Into Anno Domini lands!

Unbeknown

Man, he's trying
To shake off stupidity,
Like a dog tries
To shake off its tail.

He knows not where
               It's coming from,

Or where
            It's going.

No place, no plan,
Nothing consumed,
No waste, no time,
But too much to lose.

No place, no plan,
Something understood,
Something recognised . . .
Something unbeknown.

Thank You

For the supreme,
The unseen,
Transparencies,
Of love,
In tendency.

For the breath of life,
Of love,
The scream,
The inner vein;
And the need to escape.

The scraps of truth,
The food of love,
That I waste
And transform
Into being.

Stangelove

We have kissed in hotels,
Singing a drunken shanty,
Or mantra.
In the strong hold of Aura,
Susceptible to the skies, of belief,
Besotted by the captivity of belief.

We looked ghostly upon the sea,
Looking for an ending,
We told tales, like stars
Tell their tales of mourning.
Only lovers
Tell haunting tales.

There was indignation,
In the face of the janitor,
Who swept away your eyelashes,
Acquiescently, he prayed,
'Hosanna, is a cosseted whore,
Of Western caprice!'

No play or opus,
Could parody such a faithless spectre,
Without an iota of understanding,
Or inkling of love.
Sucking out the emptiness,
Like the sea, through a straw.

Lament To The Poet

I could redeem this Capitalist nation,
Boast of its freedom,
Play host to slavery.
Preach to high heaven,
How selfish Man can be.

The cock crows, the rising sun,
To make the promise that day will come,
He curses, threatens to wake everyone,
Un-penned, untrue, the day will come,
We will run into the wilderness.

Heathen, love, it took a lifetime,
To overcome, controversy, beyond belief;
Of odourless airs, and howling winds;
Cause angels wings to flap furiously.
How die they! Our inspirations!

Liber Free

How insane.
How insincere,
How insipid.
To identify with sanity,
Becomes the ramblings,
Of another, saintly!

EXTOL (unsaintly)
Excoriate the boundary,
Of assurance,
Day come, day go.
Enunciate the indolent, the undead,
FREE!

Nefarious, to be hypnotised, here,
Defeated, are we, from one
To another,
In defence, in defiance;
My demise
In exemption.

LIBER FREE!
LIBER FREE!
THE LIGHT! THE DARK!
LIBER FREE!
EXTOL. WILDERNESS.

The Calico Veil

Though we were born to proximity,
It is not near enough,
To know in thee, the word of love,
Embellished is the dream.
To swallow all daemons'
Seed, and sow the convolutions
Of evolution, its remedies.

How I hope to surpass these pits of dream,
And hiss, the notes of my pitch,
In night, they order these streams
That flow in my veins.
How I escaped!
To clamber from the queue,
That waits for us to dream again.

The calling, the sermon, the calico veil,
I was summoned to witness,
My very fate, as if I were traitor,
Or preface to the death of love;
Or lover of pride, become, that,
To which men fell and died!
Called it fate, called it pride.

The Complicity Of My Shadow

It was on a night like this,
With all its razzmatazz,
To sup the juice of forever,
I sang my smile for you; like this;

It was on a night like this,
With all redemption,
I rang the silent bell of honour,
A tribute to you, my father.

It was on a night like this,
I knew exactly reality,
Where all thought unnecessary,
Peeled away laughing, like crazy.

This night, the stars fell,
And lovers found strength.
This night the silent bells,
Eavesdropped in the shadows.

Wild Horses

If God should open this lifeless form,
The ghost to sprawl his name,
Upon the granite grave,
The weather beaten soul in me.

It is not privilege, so scorned,
Of wealth, acquired of power,
Of the heart and ability,
To look inside love!

I had looked too deep,
I had no other disguises, to explain,
That I am a woman,
Or a creature you despise.

Yet so exposed, I could not tell,
How cherished or unaccomplished,
Was my soul,
Of wild horses?

To The Beast, And Regard

This beast of which you speak,
The destruction of the HOLY
LANDS to pomp and circumstance,
Come, thought can make an honest man,
That he take a bow;
In his right hand,
Is his command,
His left hand may deny him,
As in prayer he plays,
With execution,
And judgement makes of him,
Superior! Sport!

But prayer comes to circumstance,
And thought,
As you blush your innocence,
Irresponsible you become,
Thoughtless,
And without a word,
You make regard,
To he who is judged more pure.
To he who is judged most pure,
To the superior throne,
The unequivocal, till beast and privilege,
The leopard and the lamb.

Set Sail Love!

He did not disturb the oceans,
Or cause pollution,
He could not believe
I could play this hand!

In all likelihood,
He came with muzzles,
He came with hounds,
He hustled for the carcass.

In each kiss,
He took my breath
And sold it,
To the nearest bandit!

The disgrace,
The unjustness,
My superstitious talismans
Cannot save me now.

The curse upon the land,
The stealth of love,
This fathomless, sorry sea,
Will not devour me!

The Heart

Did I believe I could extinguish flame?
All hell from hearts,
Those who flock toward the edge
Of Love, who has many daemons.

I could pray there,
For none other,
To feed my hunger,
And relish my pride.

Come on, be brave,
Beware, the path
Is narrow and crumbling,
The sea, beneath, very deep.

I will bring conclusion,
I will bring emblems,
Along by-ways, I will walk,
In the land of the heart, and its gravity.

The Firecracker

Pallid, monistic void inside,
They are critical of me,
Because I am an assassin
Of honourable men.

Prerequisite to civilisation,
I stood proud as Liberty,
My presence felt in heaven,
When I vomited on the feudal feet of the master.

'I'm no lap-dog', I sneered,
When love uttered the shallow sham
Of precision's scrimshaw destiny,
I hoarded my desire in the vault

No one to witness my inner fervour,
Favours the baited breaths, sing,
The power of the inspired
Deos volente libertine.

Traitor, they slandered,
My sanity revoked, till irrupting,
Rhetorical pressure, brought Kingdom come.
The Firecracker was my name.

Freedom

Heaven is a messenger,
The sweet honey of your soul;
Prelude to the ancient, supernatural world,
Inspiration and wile.
Take heed! An uncertain peace of the mind,
Time the base upon which order is placed,
To pacify the unrelenting mind,
Bring to heel ambition,
Make prey,
. . . Of her impression.

They gag and make mute, the multitude
Of souls, who gather in their identities,
The foolhardy, the infatuated and keen
As machines, hot headed and frenzied,
Come horsemen, in exasperation, in steed,
To fulfil need and make plea of their mockery,
The fascinate, and alluding beauty,
Of loyalty, in apparition,
Of temptation – the magnate!

They gag and make mute the innocent,
In lies are bred, suggestible,
Cavernous mind, the chasms;
The hired gun, in blood and command
The war is never-ending, no barter at all!
Peace come, that you sell another man's soul,
To save your own. A paean:
Should you serve your spirit well;
Imagine him saintly, a sage,
In prudence serve him like a nobleman.

If a man, in pseudo-psyche,
Transgression, find justice!
The craving, the deceit in difference,
That routs the light from the heart,
To indifference, and make believe,
His cryptic mind, his regal rank,
Can resist the vantage point?
To stir in him, his cold heart,
Demand and perpetuate the thing!

'In Regard'

. . . And when you held me,
I felt tied and bound, and love
Leaves a taste
Of a bad explanation,
Without word,
A cruel resolution,
A contagion of intemperate
Regard . . .

. . . Regard . . . how slight,
To compare your grace,
My gracelessness.
His face, complimented,
The collaborate,
The alter ego,
Thoughtless,
And in childish sleep . . .
Restless . . .

You should consider,
In an intelligent manna,
To ego, then, crawls,
Supplemented in rags,
My soul,
My needs denied,
To regard . . .
Planet Earth . . .

Love.

Man Of Stone

It is little told,
How heavy, his head in his hands,
His concrete clouds,
How carved he
His intimacy.

I thought myself free,
I thought I was a man of my word,
There is dust in my pockets,
The king is calling!

Dust in my veins, in my gullet,
It is more than I can do,
To keep the dust from my heart,
Turning me to stone.
Faster than the spell is cast . . .

Faster than a speeding bullet.

It does not mean a damn thing,
How dreams and demons,
Fall like white stars,
That the spell is cast,
Ill-fated.

Your dreams and your demons,
No matter how ill-fated grievance,
How, carved is intimacy,
Into stone,
Nothing new! Pygmalion,

His quarry of dreams.

Marguerite

Her prosaic liturgies
Malinger
On the bright side.

Of perdition,
Hors de Combat,
Pursuit has no reason.

It is a spurring sputter
Condones,
Starkness as this.

Levitate the mysteries,
To Marguerite, her loveliness,
Her pearls, and seeds.

Her optimism,
Screaming, 'Habdab's,
They are radiant as fish eggs!'

Heart Of Stone

Outside in the wilderness,
I heard of a creature obscured by desire.

Inside was ex-planetary.

Many prisoners had paraded
Through the story,
For identification,
I bowed to the occasion,
But yearned for more.

'Let fall not to want,' said one,
'Lay down your lust
And you will soon be free,
Lie with it, and you will remain, encaged.'
His sentence had paid its toll;
He left and returned to his cell.

Bewildered! I cried,
I ran to the creature, to ask of Fantasy;
'If your soul craved the savage
In your dreams,
Would you caress his cruel heart?'

Without hesitation, I answered,
'In my dreams I could make the heart of passion,,
Not of savage.'
'Is it not passion which drives the savage?'
'Yes, but it is cruel!'

The creature asked to see my heart,
Though reluctant, I felt the desire
To trust.
I took my heart into my hands
And held it out for him to see.
'My child! You are disoriented!'

Disarrayed that he could tell me no more,
I hid it quickly under a stone,
'Can you show me yours?' I asked.
Perplexed and angry, he sent me away.

I returned the next day,
To look for the savage,
But he was no longer there,
In his place,
In the wilderness,
Stood the prisoner.

He urged my attention,
'That creature is savage,
You should be beware,
For he is uncivilised,
Even in his innocence,
He will eat your heart!'

I ran to the stone,
My heart had gone,
But there was no pain,
For who could bear blame
Upon the savage, in his passion.

I took the stone to remind me.

Ineffected

Nightmare,
Pure equine,
At the borderline,
I defend my space.
Come the gaggle,
The peerless rent,
Of the ineffective
Pummelling,
Of didactic
Deference.

It encumbers me,
Unfulfilling,
A failed illusion,
Victims, ill-judged;
Nascence,
The mead of sense,
To represent,
Such sacristy,
Justifiably.

Rise To Dawn

When we rise to dawn,
Shall we love one another then?
As wait we for war
To subside,
And respond to peacekeeping,
War to peace become.

When we rise to dawn,
Shall we love one another then?

To litigate the devil,
His own combat,
Within reason,
In solution, war, to peace become . . .

When we rise in the morning,
Shall we love each other then?

In visions, in skies of difference,
Differential come to know,
From difference, there comes respect,
Each and every one, unsuspecting . . .

When we rise with the sun,
Will we love each other then?

When in contention for every thought,
No difference, no martyrdom,
War in contention,
War has been and gone!

Will we love one another then?

Spilt Milk

Make measure of the boot liquor,
The spilt elixirs of the soul
The kind of mixture,
Sold on the edge of trails.

Should you fall over the horizon,
Or laugh at Columbus,
Greet me at your discretion,
Fall froward into gravity.

Stand sturdy, hold strong your raft,
Find proof in heaven and the sea,
From mists, emerge not, from fatality,
Hold on sturdy.

Be courageous of the foolish,
This voyage, from which, you may never return,
Could come the end of the world!
Be silently brave.

Calm the beating seas of your heart,
With essence, do not be stricken,
These seas, could pull the ship apart,
With duty, with heroism.

Keep high the mast, steady direction,
Take, even unto death, the wild winds,
Till comes gentle the high sea,
Light of dawn, calm the unpredictable deep.

How seem the winds, never-ending,
Lift the threat and make retreat,
The whirl of the fathoms beneath,
Find control of the chaos within.

If such a tale you tell,
How brave your soul?
When explore you, the seas,
The existence of eternity.

A Day Lost

I scrutinise every gesture,
I ask why?
Should I not incite,
To ask why?

I will not speak evil
Of those who tried
To speak evil,
'til rectified . . .

Is hate the vortex of the world?
Betrothed, tactically sold,
The truth? Dear God,
I thought I knew

What I don't know now,
Such I have heard of evil,
Unknown, how can the truth be told,
In irreverence.

It's just one day lost
To the vortex of gravity,
That cast lusts
Asunder, a bold actor!

Liana

Gown me with your mercy,
Like a regent king,
Hold fast the day,
Let Fata Morgana sing.

Let not blench or blazon,
Would be a blessing,
With herald or trumpet,
Gasp the magic's clarion.

Clamant helot,
Moon Cernuous, the boatman's call,
Drink from my cup,
Absorb these rays of aura.

The deciduous scandal,
Receptivity I recall,
To all, I ever saw before me, premonition,
The description and insignia of Liana.

Prehension

Could collision in Time,
Between stars, make sublime,
Space seas, reinvent the world,
How and what we see, the consciousness,
To adapt to sphere, to reality,
Expounded and surrounded the truth, no matter
How precious, to obey, our outer being.

We could all be, consciously,
In memory, lost in time,
Or hiding in unseen dimensions of time,
But to feel as real as any dream, what it seems
To the mind, human being, the obstinate fool,
Believes ever to make sense,
Of the destiny, that awaits him.

Knowledge

Did I make fool of every gesture?
Did I dance to fool you? The Shrew,
Never a word, from her I know,
The dream is a dream
Of the universe, universal.
Of common man.

I made thirst of sorrow!
That nothing, nothing,
Would speak so
Darkly.
And deep in the heart, dark
Of understanding, I believed!

The flag is flying,
Stars and stripes,
Stars and skies,
And how I loved you,
So, the dream to dream;
Seeing is believing!

On The Verander

I believe the Virginia sunrise is beautiful!
It's surprise, it's eternity.
I am sure,
You would say, 'That is beautiful!'

When inclined,
Towards the spectacular,
The rhetoric horn of nature,
Of perfection . . . I could see . . .

Mist in the wings of morning,
When winter comes, less explained,
A drunken subterfuge,
Fears allayed, deep as the sea.

I believe the Virginia sunrise is beautiful,
Love as eternity, shines on
In my soul.
You would say, 'This is beautiful!'

I Sanctify I

Would you be the judge of this?
It was love well spent,
Metallic like the night
In armour came,
My consciousness comes into being.

> Whether a'cross, from death
> To the beginning, from life to life,
> Interposed, with voices of the dark,
> Speak to me again,
> As if strangers.

I make no promises, I put pen to paper,
That opens these hollow recesses
And places, I can hardly find,
Good-riddance, of peace, speak,

> These ruinous souls.
> Of darkness, make allegiance to them,
> Who can make spoils as if treasures,
> Temple, invaders,
> Make ridicule of belief,
> Of conscious thought.

I make dance and speak your name,
I sanctify my own being,
King of king believe me,
I defined I,
I defined in sanity.

> To defend this portion,
> In tribulation undefined,
> Somehow, my love survived.
> If I defined my cherished thought,
> As sanctity.

I Remove My Armour

Do you think me fool?
To gird all loss
Of belief, my belief in me.
That I should encapsulate the supreme,
Then see,
My surprise
When I pounced upon the offering
Of love, like a feast.

I was misconceived,
Or at least conceived selfishly,
Of reality,
That I could dictate to love.
In proviso of need,
I repeat an apology
For my fallibility,
That love is lost.

And lost again,
When I formed,
In result, by demand,
That bellowed in scorn,
Across this land.
Such pleasure, I made,
Gift of the sky,
And I advocated,
'It is invisible to the naked eye.'

Just A Man

Incredulous,
In strung up emotion,
Unto reason, find why
A man becomes hunter and hunted,
A pack dog,
A malignant fantasy of error,
Obsequious obscenities.

And what, your sacrifice?
What your gift?
Make outcry in insignificance,
In relation, hostile boundary,
Militancy, magnificent mystery,
Established,
Sense of life!

Intuitive, to perdition,
Recall, associate,
Cognizance of the soul,
Unfold rare, and majestic,
Silence, cowers,
To breeding,
Wily yarns of rude discourse.

Impervious an acumen,
Comes to wake man in his dawn,
And in wakefulness, a wilderness,
He renounces his worthiness,
To a void,
Of nothingness
And impression.

In restraint and immodest,
To flummox my heart and pulse
To race,
The tempo, in affect,
Over charged,
And outraged my heart,
My pulse, my veins, lifeless.

Vexed to furore, temperament
In lifeless shadows dance,
Forecast the past
As if tomorrow
You will live,
Life to life, dust to dust.

The ignominy of prevalence,
Out of this God forsaken world,
On the frontier of this worship,
Your eminence.
The charade,
Concealed in cruel and brutal
Command, He's just a man.

Paean

By deed is done!
They are less than warriors,
Extraneous and direct,
In control.

And by deed is done!
Circumstance, and faith,
Erodes and makes extract
Of soul.

Pomp! In certainty,
Makes a ghostly muse of me,
Confounded and confused.
The Paean!

Heathen, Christian, Jew, Muslim,
Apollo, soulful,
Make ease, put down your guns.
Carefree, is death upon me?

A Maze/d

To belittle my wisdom,
To your own conclusion;
Opprobrium,
The ceaseless expanse,
Of grandeur,
The scrutiny of heart.

Make levy the tarry,
The dilemma, the quandary,
The stamina of poverty;
The ravening rancour,
The kudos.

It was ill-conceived,
Raging and besotted,
An epithet, a whim,
A veil of conceit,
The labyrinthine.

Paler Shades Of Grey

There are solutions,
Deep in your soul,
(You know you well!)
Impulse, the sound
Of your ambition;
Comes more to confusion,
Interference and intention,
With-held conclusion.

I don't think
It would surprise me!
Thought, a paler shade
Of grey.

From rapid to slow and lazy thoughts,
From easy days, to enlightened moons,
In rain, when rained rain,
Like you had never seen
In the light of day,
In the pale, pale, morning,
It rained like rain could rain,
A fire within me, I thought,
Extinguished, but still
Burning.

It rained,
In a paler shade of grey,
Pale, paler than imagined,
Still the fire burned.

Inscription And Spell

So soul; know well, your soul,
Take the elements
Blow them to the winds,
Bring the truth, bring your being,
Bring your magical stones.

Conceive the sphere of earth
And moon, in creation,
Your soul,
So follow your shadows,
Genesis and Assiah.

To have need
Of mentor, akin
To comparison, Eulogy,
Praise and homage,
His happy hunting ground.

In rapture,
Seventh Heaven,
Does praise his reform,
His exception, his muse,
Send him home wearily.

The Courage Of Lady Godiva

You're a Romeo,
I'm your defeat.
Come an errant knight,
Gallant,
Of the spiked black night.

These things I collect,
As if in churlish witchcraft,
Make bow and arrow,
And to the sky make aim,
Of love and chancery.

He would come in
A'galloping,
As love first shines,
Must shine to the moon.

Consciousness is in the shadows,
When naked to the world,
And they can peep,
So coldly.

Factory Of Dream

The factory swell,
I remember it well,
The homecoming tides,
The despondent.

Iron grey walls
Of emphatic dreams,
The mealy-mouthed
Credit of truth.

In the electricity of night,
The long kiss goodnight,
From the bottom of the bottle,
Comes the compromise.

Everyone's heart,
Ripped apart,
In the bargain of escape,
The dispossessed.

Thank God,
For Alexander!

Estranged Spirit

I gave her freedom,
That she could boast;
I gave her riches,
The jealous ghost;
I gave her beauty,
The dying host.

I gave her adventure,
At deadly cost;
I gave her intelligence,
The meaning lost!
I gave her admiration,
She loved the most!
I gave her life,
It turned to dust.

Elemental Universe

Breath so faint,
It cannot be heard,
As breath by breath,
We become one.

I am vengeful of her love,
I pour all my waters,
Into restless seas, then ripples
Into havoc.

These tremors reach the outer edges of the galaxy,
Her laughter evaporates into mists of love,
And the moon commands all envy,
The choirs of stars.

Sing into the sky,
With servility, the heart an epiphyte,
Of devotion,
And ghostly there . . .

The storms take refuge,
Like guardian angels who sleep
On the moon, the sycophantic universe,
Then swaggers toward Heaven.

Dream Of Peace

You croon and sing,
As the crow flies,
You ride the wind.

The finest art,
I find, your heart,
To where depart the shadows.

I fear you not,
Your kiss and your breath,
I fear not.

Such loneliness,
In subtle demand,
Comes faint breath.

Distant the piano.

In the laughter,
My sweet sister,
A little speechless, a little unknown.

Impression

How is cast the eye
Over the impression.
Devoured, darkened
To everlasting retreat,
My sleep.

With such disbelief.
Saddened with grief,
I cannot contend,
For my soul, beat,
I could not contend.

The game!
This contentious grip,
Cruelty, you made me weep;
Beg to be seen;
Beggar's belief.

The voice, unheard,
Disheartened, my mind,
Falling into the deep,
Darkened night,
Of my sleep.

His silent cloak around me,
My consciousness numb
To the world,
Death, for a moment,
Was easy.

Indifference

As in position, a star, then
Came reaction, exposed,
Position in space, less expected;
The Hydra upon them!

In the capitol, in deep inner space,
In plagues of war, it was committed of them,
Less than man could suppose,
All within, wasted, to indifference.

In all within, in the sense of things,
I take hold, my obedience,
I have tamed it at last!
Then came, the Final Judgement, of man.

Of men, less loved, than condemned,
To the sense of beloved, content,
He should be loved less!
Than lost to indifference.

In Every Stroke Of Hand

The exalted,
Could dance,
Upon the sighted
Stage of trance,
And make swoon,
The spirit of age,
Dance inside you.

To indulge
In impression,
To touch you,
To bring omen's;
Dare devils,
Of love's infusions.

In A Man's Eyes

You look like a hungry man;
A tear away heart,
Spellbound.
A merciless man;
Lay down your hand,
Lay down your hand.

Spine-chilling love,
Unseen dream,
My impressions,
A metaphor;
I'm in a daze,
I'm in a daze.

Here's my peace offering,
Soldier;
I'm a little older,
I got a little wise;
And I can see the colour
Of any man's eyes.